THE RABBI'S
TOUCH

Ten Encounters
with Jesus that
Changed Everything

ANNETTA LAMMERS

THE RABBI'S TOUCH
Copyright © 2020 by Annetta Lammers

Author photo by April Voorberg

The information contained within is intended to encourage and inspire, but it is not a substitute for direct and considered reading of the Bible.

Unless otherwise noted, all Scripture quotations are from The Holy Bible, English Standard Version® (ESV®), copyright © 2001 by Crossway, a publishing ministry of Good News Publishers. Used by permission. All rights reserved. Scripture quotations marked AMPC are quotations taken from the Amplified® Bible (AMPC), Copyright © 1954, 1958, 1962, 1964, 1965, 1987 by The Lockman Foundation Used by permission. www. Lockman.org

Print ISBN: 978-1-4866-1983-2
eBook ISBN: 978-1-4866-1984-9

Word Alive Press
119 De Baets Street, Winnipeg, MB R2J 3R9
www.wordalivepress.ca

WORD ALIVE
—P R E S S—

Cataloguing in Publication may be obtained through Library and Archives Canada

CONTENTS

INTRODUCTION

A field is a perfect place to meet Jesus. Green grass, a shade tree, cool breezes, and the sound of water rippling through a nearby stream. Add an invitation to sit, and one knows he or she will be fed. It's the perfect place for a picnic, a conversation, a friendship.

Early in his gospel, the disciple John tells the story of Jesus feeding the five thousand. It was a large crowd, thousands of individuals who spent the day seeking and searching for Jesus. Regardless of their reasons for being there, they finally found Jesus at the end of the day, when they were tired and hungry and had no food.

It says in Scripture, *"Jesus went up on the mountain, and there he sat down with his disciples" (John 6:3)*. And, *"Jesus said, 'Have the people sit down.' Now there was much grass in the place" (John 6:10a)*.

Notice that both the crowds and Jesus sat down. Right here we will find a hint of a hidden gem. From a seated position, Jesus watched this large, eager crowd approach Him. That word *sat* in this passage comes from the Greek word *kathemai*, which means "to be seated, as in dwell, enthroned, reside". The root of *kathemai* is *kata*, which means "down from a higher to a lower plane". The Greek meaning behind *sat* suggests that the person performing this action is one who sits on a throne and is coming down from a higher position.

As He is seated, waiting and watching with authority, John tells us that Jesus asks the disciples to invite the people to sit down as well. However, (and this is what is so delightful about God's Word), here the word for *sit* is the Greek word *anapipto*, which means "to fall back, or to lie down, recline (at a dinner-table) or fall back upon (the breast of another person reclining at dinner)". Isn't that exactly what Jesus invites us to do, to fall back on him for a meal and conversation?

A most wonderful detail is given by John in this story. Verse 10 tells us that the crowd was invited to recline on grass. And not just a little bit of grass, but "much grass", a field of grass. The Greek word for grass is *chortos,* which means "a feeding place, food, grass, herbage". A feeding place! The layers of repetition are not by accident. The Lord and Master, the one who came from a higher place and lowered Himself to the place of His created, invites them for a meal in a lush feeding place and provides that meal in abundance.

As you read these stories of Jesus, recline, nestle into the grass, and lean back on Him. Settle in to meet Him in the lives of the people on the following pages. Join those who also fell on Him, who needed to lean on Him for their desperate needs, to feel his touch.

Matthew 8:16, 17 says, *"That evening they brought to him many who were oppressed by demons, and he cast out the spirits with a word and healed all who were sick. This was to fulfill what was spoken by the prophet Isaiah: 'He took our illnesses and bore our diseases'."*

Jesus is available for all who come. Sometimes that's all He wants and all we can do—come to Him and fall on Him.

Unveiled

I call upon you, for you will answer me, O God;
incline your ear to me; hear my words.

—Psalm 17:6

The blind man sat at the side of the road. He knew his place, a place known by many. Daily, it was his lot to find that hollow near the road where he was far enough back to not be trampled. So many people on that road, going in and out of Jericho. What were they doing? What was their hurry? The endless scuffle of sandals, the earthy smell of donkeys, horses, and other animals, the yelling and shoving that occasionally happened, and the billows of dust. The dust. That was why he wore the cloak. The garment was a shelter and hiding place from the dust and dirt. If needed, he could grab it to cover his mouth as he hunkered down for the day beneath its shelter. The cloak—all he had, really—made the hollow a bit more bearable.

He only saw dark, never light. The days of seeing light were a vague memory. The memory of loss. Though he could no longer enjoy it with his eyes, the heat of the sun on his head told him that the light was there, all around him. He could time how long he'd been sitting at the road's edge by where the heat felt the most intense.

In the cooler hours of the morning, he noticed the heat on his feet, nearest the road. That was the time to be more attentive to the faithful generous who would throw a few coins in front of him. His cloak would catch and muffle the clink, but he recognized the sound. By noon, the shade of the sycamore tree behind him would begin to creep up his back. He guessed the tree to be well advanced in years, having grown familiar with the exposed roots that cupped his form day after day.

Though the memories of having vision were faint, the longing to see again could be intense at times. To keep from losing his mind, he learned to divert his thoughts and accept his lot. "The blind man" was his station in Jericho. Many took pity on him and tossed him coins. One faithfully led him to his spot each morning—if he roused himself in time. Yet, he couldn't completely bury that desire to see again. Sometimes it would rise up with a painful grip on his heart, and he needed to force it back down, reminding himself sternly about the reality of his situation.

His ears worked fine, but people talked as though he didn't hear either. He heard things. And something he'd been hearing a lot lately was a name: Jesus. Words drifted on the cool morning breeze or on the quiet evening air, landing like hope. Jesus... a rabbi and master teacher with authority. Jesus fed five thousand men and their families with only two fish and five loaves of bread. The words were whispered with wonder. Jesus... lepers cleansed. A woman touched his hem and became healed and clean. But the whispers that filled his whole being with intense hope—a man born blind... Jesus put mud on his eyes… told him to go to the pool… now he can see. Can see! Those words echoed in his heart.

Who was this man who touched and healed? Who turned back time to restore sight? Who taught and fed the crowd? If he heard the stories right, whoever He was, He did these things with a touch and a word. When He spoke, His words carried authority like no other. What would His touch feel like? His voice sound like?

More words travelled to him like a ripple on the wind. Jesus was in Jericho. An intensity of emotion threatened to overwhelm him. Jesus was near? In Jericho? Would He come this way?

The minutes crawled by slowly, until it felt as though the sun was nearly directly overhead. Despair nipped at him. What if he missed the Rabbi? The dust and din grew. A large crowd moved toward him. His heart beat faster, and he sat up straight beneath his cloak. Agitated, he blurted to those nearby, "Is He here?"

The reply filled the air around him. "Yes, He is here!"

Jesus. The blind man's longing and hope burst out of his throat. A cry. A scream. "Jesus, Son of David, have mercy on me!" Deep inside him, a desperate yearning to be healed rose. This teacher, this healer, he could give him his sight. And now Jesus was close. He cried out louder, "Jesus! Son of David, have pity and compassion on me."

A harsh voice rebuked him. "Stop calling the Master. He is busy. He is on His way to Jerusalem and is in a hurry. He has no time for one such as you." Other voices piled on him, threatening to drown out his hope, even the knowledge of his belief. But no. He wouldn't let Jesus pass. The blind man shrieked louder, insisting on encountering Jesus and His healing hand. He shouted desperately above the rebukes, the insistence that Jesus was too busy, the fears that this was all he was good for in life—begging. He cried out above the jostling and noise and dust, "Son of David, have mercy on me!"

Suddenly, a stillness wrapped around the crowd. In that pause he heard the command, "Call him."

Then hands reached for him and those around him spoke encouraging words, "Take heart and get up! He is calling you."

All the hope and longing that had been building inside him coursed through the blind man's veins as courage. The now-burdensome cloak fell to the ground as he leaped to his feet and lurched toward the direction of the commanding voice. Hands guided him through the crowd toward Jesus.

When those guiding him directed him to stop, the crowd's voices faded. The man's opaque eyes searched. Was he standing in front of the Rabbi?

"What do you want Me to do for you?" The question was quiet, compassionate. The blind man shifted his gaze towards that beaconing voice, filled with compassion and power, extending him permission to speak his desire. Encouraging him to believe that he could have again what he had lost.

Boldly and earnestly the man said, "Master, Rabbi, let me have my sight back."

Through the longing, he heard Jesus speak in a voice that quieted all his needs and questions. "Go your way, recover your sight, your faith has made you well."

That voice. Glowing light. The sun bursting into full glory. Light and blue sky and faces. All of it faded as the man's eyes settled on the face before him. Kind, warm eyes twinkling light and joy and acknowledgment. Love gazing back into his now-clear eyes. The opaque covering was gone! His heart received and was filled with that light and joy. Jesus had healed him with a few simple words, and the love the man saw in His eyes changed him further. He was known. He was no longer "the blind man" but, for the first time in many years, Bartimaeus.

Jesus calmly turned and continued on that road to Jerusalem. "Go your way", He had said, leaving Bartimaeus standing in the road in wonder and quiet worship. He fixed his restored eyes on the back of the man of healing for several minutes, until he became aware of his surroundings, the crowd brushing against him as they continued down the road after the Rabbi.

Eyes seeing, cloak left behind at the foot of that tree hollow outside Jericho, Bartimaeus followed Jesus with eyes full of light and a heart full of the ultimate Light.

No Longer Hiding

Because you are precious in my eyes,
and honored, and I love you…

—Isaiah 43:4a

So many people. The woman had never seen throngs like this before. And she hadn't considered seeking out someone in a crowd, certainly not in these past twelve years. She adjusted her head covering nervously, the soft texture a comfort to her fingers and flushed cheeks. Twelve years of unpredictable flux had made her unclean. Made everything and everyone she touched unclean.

Sadness and loneliness weighed on her at the thought of her empty days, distant conversations, the rarest of hugs. So many losses. Friends and resources gone, creating a seclusion that multiplied her pain. Dashed hopes. Throughout all these years, things had only grown worse with her monthly cycle. Month after month after month. No cure was to be had. Doctors gave only bad reports as she weakened with each cycle, her very life ebbing away in the constant and torturous flow of blood and pain. She was desperate for help. Her cries to heaven seemed to go nowhere. How could they? She was always unclean. How could an unclean woman be heard by a pure and holy God?

Then she began hearing the rumours, when she ventured out discreetly to seek the latest cure. A person here or there would share wondrous stories of a man who healed. He wasn't a doctor as she knew them. According to the stories, it only took a word or a touch from this man, this Rabbi, and people were made whole. Many had been healed while they were with Him. The multitudes would listen to his teaching and He would heal. Lepers, the paralyzed, all sorts of diseased people, men, even women and children, came and He healed them all. Willingly and with no exception. Was He the One? The One from Heaven?

The woman considered what she had heard and thought about all the doctors she had gone to. Her resources had been depleted as she followed their instructions, to no avail. Yet here was a man who healed without demanding a price, as far as she knew. The key was to go to Him. Hope battled her despair. She needed to get to this man named Jesus.

How should she approach Him? It wouldn't be an easy thing. For others, it would be as simple as finding out where He was and seeking His help, but for her, who wasn't to be around other people, it was not that straightforward. But perhaps, if she could gather her fragile courage, it could be.

Years of pain and isolation drove her to abandon her usual caution. After carefully asking about the Rabbi's location, she found herself at her present vantage point. She pressed herself against a slight outcrop, hoping to blend in, and studied the lake in the distance. It was a clear azure right now, though she knew it could hold the worst of storms and rough, grey waters, which would better match her current mood.

She'd heard that He had left to cross the lake, but He was coming back this way. Apparently many had heard the same news, and the waiting crowds were overwhelming, growing minute by minute. She had not expected that. What was she to do?

The woman shrank back a little, pulling her cloak tighter and trying to become more invisible. She was still unclean, her flux never leaving lately, only growing worse. She tried to push down the despair that threatened her at the thought that she risked breaking every law pertaining to her uncleanness. Even now she could feel the panic inside her as she considered the need for fresh rags. Still, she couldn't leave yet.

She glanced around. No one appeared to have noticed her. All attention was fixed on a boat carrying several people and slowly approaching on the calm waters. Was one of the people Jesus? Before the fishing boat reached the shore, throngs began to push towards Him, the air filling with cries of need and longing. That cry echoed her own heart and she longed to be there in that crowd.

Jesus could hardly make headway through the people. He had trouble moving but eventually He made His way up the rise, striding with purpose. Somehow a path cleared in front of him. How was that possible? She fixed her eyes on Him and the effect He had on the crowds. The crying need changed to praise and rejoicing as one after the other received what they had pleaded with him for. This man had power! But how was she to capture his attention? The obstacles seemed insurmountable. In her mind, she examined each of her options and shook her head. *Impossible.* Despair filled her, threatening to overwhelm her and leave her in a hopeless heap.

The woman's brow furrowed as she studied him. He was full of power, and nothing seemed to be outside His healing ability. Could it be that all she needed to do was touch that power? Perhaps no one needed to know. Could she secretly come up behind Him and not attract His attention? Would a simple touch do it? He wouldn't need to know it was an unclean woman touching Him. Dare she? What would happen if she was caught? She pressed a hand to her mouth. Oh, the shame and danger of being caught. She could be stoned!

The battle continued in her mind as she watched Him gradually pressing through the crowds. She needed to decide soon. Panic clouded her thinking.

She contemplated the throng. So many people pushing and shoving to get close to the healer. Yet, that could mean those in the crowd would never feel another body pressing against them. The desperation to be free, strong, and healthy grew inside her. She gazed at the man heading her way and hope surged through her like never before. A curious humility emanated from this powerful man, a sense of strength yet gentleness. He was different. Somehow she sensed that He was trustworthy, unlike the doctors out there, unlike most men. This Jesus was more than a mere man. *All I need to do is touch His garments and I'll be made whole and well.*

The woman adjusted her cloak and straightened the striped headpiece with determination. Was there any way to remove the identifying piece? The cloth screamed *Unclean.* If even one person identified it... Straightening her shoulders, she left it as it was and made her way toward the crowd, her eyes on the backs of the muted robes pressed tightly together. Spotting an opening, she gathered her robes with one hand. When she was close enough to touch the people in front of her, their eyes fixed ahead on Jesus, she crouched low and squeezed her way with quick and deft movements between legs and cloaks. Occasionally she needed to crawl on her knees to get through, yanking her robes up to keep from getting tangled. She worked to keep her eyes and thoughts on her goal so she wouldn't give up.

One of her fingers was crushed beneath a sandal and she muffled her cry of pain. Aware of her flow, she was gripped by a strong urge to flee the crowds and return to the safety and comfort of her home. The crowd surged forward, propelling her with them, and she struggled to keep her balance. It was too late to turn back.

The flitting thought of being dragged before the crowd and stoned threatened her resolve, but she drowned the thoughts with the litany in her mind, *I just need to touch His garment. I just need to touch His garment. I just need to touch His garment and I will be well.* That determination was interrupted by the ever-present need for more rags. The circling, haunting thoughts of making everyone she was brushing up against unclean clawed at her mind as the pit in her stomach grew.

She could scream from the terror. And yet, she pushed back the fear and pictured in her mind this man Jesus and touching His cloak.

The woman tried to keep her bearings by listening to what those around her were saying. Soon she sensed she was getting close to the Rabbi. A trickle of anticipation fought with the dark pit inside her. Then, through the legs, robes, and dust, she caught a glimpse of a robe with a blue fringe on it—a rabbinical fringe. It was Him! Urgency rose in her. He'd be out of reach soon. She elbowed her way through the clamouring throng, desperate to reach that robe.

With a final determined push, she stretched her hand out and felt the fringe brush over her fingertips.

Time stood still.

She held her breath as a surge of energy and strength pulsed through her body. Instantly, the sensations of her flux disappeared. Gone. She *knew* it. People shoved against her crouched form, jostling her as she froze in wonder, staring at her still-outstretched fingertips. The ones that had touched the Healer's tassels.

It struck her then, what she had done, and she began to shake uncontrollably.

The crowd shifted as she backed into the throng, still crouched low and holding her fingers tightly to her body. She had been healed, but she was still dressed as if she wasn't.

A voice spoke. Strong and gentle, with a questioning tone. "Who touched my cloak?"

She stopped, her eyes widening. He knew?

Someone standing between her and the Rabbi exclaimed, "Look at all the people and crowds. They're pressing in hard all around you. How can you notice a touch?"

The woman bit her lip. Would the healer accept that? If he did, maybe he would continue on his way and she could flee from this increasingly threatening crowd.

The heavy pause lengthened. She swallowed hard. He was looking for her. He knew what she had done. She had not escaped being found out after all.

Her trembling legs struggled to hold her up. She held her hands close to her body as she rose, fearful, from her crouched position. Gasps echoed around her as people drew back, recognizing the striped headpiece that indicated her uncleanness. The woman stood paralyzed. What would happen now? As the crowd shrank from her, they created the path she needed to approach Jesus. Head bowed, she stumbled on weak, bruised knees toward him and threw herself on the ground at his feet, fully aware that she was at His mercy.

He said nothing but made a slight move towards her as if wanting to see her better. She couldn't look at Him, let alone meet His eyes. What would she see in His gaze? Still trembling, the story poured out of her. She fixed her gaze on the dirt, hands clasping her headpiece, longing to pull it off. Even in the midst of her telling, she revelled in the awe at what had happened in her body. She didn't mince words or avoid any details. Finally, she stopped.

The quiet that followed seemed to still and thicken the air around her. Then His voice, tender yet ringing with authority, spoke over the crowd.

"Daughter."

The woman blinked. He called her *daughter*? A word so intimate? One who is precious and of great value? A word of acceptance. The wonder swept over her and she lifted her head to meet His face. His eyes bore no threat or condemnation, only love and warmth and acceptance. He *saw* her. He saw the years of exclusion and loneliness. He saw the fear, the physical pain, and great loss she had endured, and He didn't pull back like those around Him did.

"You were persuaded to trust and it has made you whole." His laugh was gentle. "You persisted in it. Go in peace and be saved from all that your torturous plague brought you."

Her body ceased its trembling and a deep peace flowed over her as the words settled in her heart. A peace she couldn't remember ever experiencing. She longed to stay in His presence with that love enveloping her. Then it sank in that, before everyone in the surrounding throng, she had been declared accepted and whole, no longer unclean.

The woman's fingers tugged at the edges of the offending headpiece. She was anxious to remove it but thought it better to leave her hair covered. As soon as she was home, she could take it off forever. Her fingers stilled and she laughed a small laugh as she gazed at her Healer. Eyes twinkling, He nodded a blessing before turning to continue on His mission.

The crowds flowed around her as she stood in wonder, brushing up against robes and neighbours without reservation. She was free.

BREAD CRUMBS

Up to this time you have not asked a [single] thing
in My Name [as presenting all that I Am];
but now ask and keep on asking and you will receive,
so that your joy (gladness, delight) may be full and complete.
—John 16:24, AMPC

Leaning over the dough, she pounded it into submission, expressing all her fears and frustration. Glancing over her shoulder, she contemplated her daughter resting on the bed— for now. They had endured an awful night of wrestling and battling, her arms wrapped around her little daughter so she wouldn't hurt herself in all the thrashing. Such a petite thing, yet, when taken over by that evil force, almost too strong to hold still. The child had finally fallen asleep that morning out of exhaustion, but it was obvious that *that thing,* that demon, was still there by the way her little body twitched and muttered groans came out of her mouth.

The mother was exhausted too, body and soul, weary with fighting, weary of the fear and worry, weary of the constant vigilance to protect her daughter. Her husband was gone for weeks on end, as he needed to go where the work was. The weight of caring for their daughter rested on her shoulders, but she could see the weariness in him, too. He worked hard but felt helpless to help her or their daughter.

She had a brief respite in making their day's bread, and she used the physical exertion and the repetition of kneading and pounding to try and rid herself of the overwhelming terror and questions a night like last night always brought. Would it ever end? Despair clawed at her, making her nauseated. Doctors—if that's what they were—and religious leaders all had their opinion and treatments. None worked, and now she tried to hide her daughter in her home. It was hard to hide the screams, though. Thankfully, she had kind neighbours who kept their distance yet tried to help in their own way.

The woman studied her daughter. So tiny. Too tiny. Frail and thin with large eyes staring at her, silently pleading with her to make it all stop. That dark thing inside her was stealing all her life and growth, slowly killing her sweet daughter. She used to play so freely, dark curls blowing in the breeze as she twirled in the cloak her mother had worn as a child. The woman could picture it in her mind, and the memory brought sadness. How long since any of them had danced?

Then, those eyes begging for help would change. As though that *thing* stared back at her, dark and empty and all shadows. And the next battle would begin. How could she make it stop? As the woman carried her flatbread to the hot stone to bake, she screamed inside. *Who can make it stop?! Who?* She desperately needed someone to help.

Rumors had been circulating lately about a Rabbi from Israel. According to the stories, any who came to Him were healed. The weary mother crouched in front of the stone, rocking back on her heels. She'd heard of their God, Yahweh she thought His name was. An unseen God who was a mixture of holiness, justice, and compassion.

Strange, the things that came to her memory now. What of the tale of that boy healed of a violent demon? Neighbours had been quick to share that story. Maybe to encourage her? Instead, it filled her with despair. How was she to bring her daughter to a Healer when she was a foreigner and a woman? Both made her anathema to those in Israel. She knew the strict boundaries. Why offer hope if it was unattainable? Roughly, she turned the flatbread on the stone. Crumbs fell into the coals and she inhaled a burnt odor. Loss, waste. She almost broke down and cried. Yet, she knew if she started there may be no end to the tears that would surely turn to unrestrained weeping.

A timid knock at the door interrupted her spiralling thoughts. One of the neighbours? They were always so careful when approaching their home. The woman smoothed her clothing as she straightened, forcing a calm expression onto her face. After a quick glance at her daughter assured her the child was still resting, the woman relaxed her hunched shoulders and approached the door.

When she opened it part way, her neighbour from down the road peered furtively into the room. The tall, kind-faced woman adjusted her robe slightly before speaking in a hushed but urgent whisper, "He's here."

Though a vague statement, the mother's heart seemed to momentarily stop. She *knew* who her neighbour meant—the Rabbi.

Her neighbour confirmed her thought. "The Healer from Israel is here!" She described a house around the corner from the large sycamore tree and not far from their homes. "He just arrived, and I knew you would want to know." The tall woman stepped back as if eager to leave, now that her message was given.

The mother shot out a hand and grabbed her neighbour's arm, "Don't go."

Thoughts raced through her head as she took a deep, shaky breath. Her heart pounded with hope—a fierce desire to fight for the deliverance of her daughter, of their family. Somehow she knew that, if anyone could take care of a demon, this man could.

Pushing back her overwhelming emotions, she asked, "Please, would you stay with my daughter? She's resting. If she awakes, simply hold her and assure her that I'm not far and all will be well." She pushed the door open wider.

The neighbour hesitated, glancing nervously between her and the darkened doorway. When her eyes met the mother's, she must have seen the determination there, because she stood a bit taller and stepped inside, taking her own deep breath. She looked around the home until she focussed on the fragile girl, lost amidst the sheets on the bed. Compassion crossed her face and she held out a hand toward the door. "Yes, you must go. Quickly!"

The woman grabbed her cloak and dashed out the door. Throwing it around her shoulders, she ran toward the sycamore. Perhaps she should walk and present herself as dignified for the Healer, but she didn't care. Her heart overflowed and the years of emotion and need and desperation built as she flew along the few streets to the home where she would find Him. She spotted the sycamore tree and lifted her robe to avoid stumbling in her eagerness. As she approached the open door of the home, she could no longer hold her emotions in check.

The cry that tore out of her carried all of her pain and sorrow and need. In a voice that didn't sound like hers, she uttered the garbled words, "Have mercy on me. O Lord, have mercy!"

Reaching the house, she cried out even louder, "O Lord, Son of David, my daughter…" She gulped back a sob as she stopped in the doorway. "My daughter is extremely oppressed and vexed by a demon."

Silence.

The mother refused to be deterred or dismissed. She continued crying out, "O Lord, have mercy!" The words tore out of her in an urgent scream, tears streaming down her cheeks and dripping from her chin as she peered into the house.

A group of men were gathered around the One she assumed was the Healer. He was reclining, resting, and her heart gave a twinge. Clearly, He was tired. Still, her cries continued unhindered as the years of fear and pain and sorrow poured out. The men were likely His followers, and they winced at her cries. They spoke His name, Jesus, as they begged Him to send her away. Obviously they loved and respected Him, and wanted Him to rest.

Despair consumed her. She was a mere woman, a foreigner. Why would a man of such authority listen to her? Why would He care about her daughter? Surely the requests of His followers would have preference.

Then He turned to her, his face partly in shadow. She tightened her grip on the doorframe. "I was only sent as a messenger to those who are lost in Israel."

Her throat went dry. He had spoken to her! Her despair lifted. Even if His words weren't encouraging, He hadn't immediately turned her away. That emboldened her to enter the home, and she flew the last few steps and fell on her face at His feet. All she could get out around a sob of hope was, "Lord, help me!"

The Rabbi answered, "It is not good to take the bread that belongs to the children and cast it to the dogs." Her heart sank. Who was she? A Canaanite. A woman. She knew He was right, yet...

"Yes, Lord," she murmured as she continued to bow before Him in reverence, contemplating His words.

It took the rest of her dwindling courage to raise her bowed head, but her heart stilled when she met gentle, tired eyes filled with fire. She knew what she was asking was much, but instinctively felt that a little from this man would be enough. *The crumbs.* "Even the dogs eat the crumbs that fall from the master's table."

His eyes, kind before, now filled with an even greater warmth and tenderness that washed over her.

"Yes!" He exclaimed with a smile that melted the tiredness away and revealed the strength of that fire within. "O, Woman, you have great faith! Because of that statement, you may go home and find your daughter well. The demon has left her."

Tears drying on her face, she gathered her cloak as she rose, her heart pounding to the rhythm of joy. Smiling her gratitude and an acknowledgement of His work, she turned and left the home. Once beyond the threshold, she lifted her robes around her knees and raced up the street, not letting herself question or doubt, only eager to see her daughter free and whole.

Curious neighbours poked their heads out of windows and doorways, watching her joyful dash. Finally she reached her home and flew through the door. Her daughter was still in bed but different. No darkness, simply resting, fully at peace. Chest rising gently with each restoring breath. A glow and vibrancy beginning to shine on her little face.

The mother glanced at her waiting neighbour, who smiled and held out the forgotten bread, still warm and rescued from the coals.

FORGIVEN

Bless the Lord, O my soul,
and forget not all his benefits,
who forgives all your iniquity,
who heals all your diseases…

—Psalm 103:2-3

The man, limbs thin under his robe, lay on his mat under a tree by the Capernaum gate. Friends had carried him there so he could collect alms. Every day was the same. The same mat, dull with years of use. The same dusty location with meager shade and smells of the sea. The same feet and faces rushing past without a glance, a few pausing faithfully to drop a few coins his way. The same body that refused to even sit up. And the same thoughts running through his mind. *Why…* and *if only…*

As he lay there, lost in his darkening thoughts, awareness slowly seeped in. Something was different that morning. What was it? A flash of a black robe caught his attention and then another, passing without hesitation. Pharisees? What were they doing here in Capernaum? Something was causing a stir and, now that he was paying attention, he observed that those passing by him were engaged in animated discussions. The words "Rabbi" and "Jesus" wafted his way.

As he was trying to sort it out, four robes in a variety of colours and quality blocked his view. "Jesus is here," someone gasped, out of breath. A familiar voice declared, with conviction, that their friend needed to be taken to this Jesus. And, as they had done on so many occasions, four pairs of hands grasped the leather straps on the four corners of his mat and gently, but firmly, lifted the worn mat. After settling him in the middle of the mat, his faithful friends jostled their way through the gate and toward the centre of the town, the man swaying between them.

His thoughts whirled. Where were they taking him? He tried to voice the question, but his friends shushed his doubts and wonderings while they laboured in their carrying. They were determined, and he could sense that difference in how they carried him. Their steps contained a bounce and they laughed occasionally. They were enjoying this! One of his friends craned his neck to speak over his shoulder, "Friend, Jesus will heal you!"

Heal? After all these years and after what he'd done? No. Only God could do that. And why would He when the man didn't deserve it? The familiar weakness in his body overwhelmed him.

"Why Jesus?" he finally got out.

Tall and with a broad grin, the first man exclaimed, "Where have you been? Haven't you heard? This man is healing everyone who comes to Him. The sick and any who were demon-oppressed He healed right there outside Peter's house not long ago. Now He's back in Capernaum. You don't want to miss this."

No, he hadn't heard… Such dark thoughts had crowded his mind lately. Dismay crept in as he swayed on his mat, battling the contagious excitement of his four friends who were so eager to care for him.

The second man added, with awe in his voice, "I've heard that He teaches like He has the power to act on what He says. As though He's from God. I think it's getting the Scribes and Pharisees worked up." He chuckled quietly, beneath his beard.

That explained the dignified robes. The man tried to look around from his swinging mat to see if there were any black robes on the streets. But the streets appeared a bit quieter than they had been, and his friends picked up their pace, seeming to fly over the streets in their eagerness. What was he to do with this?

His friends slowed down, appearing to hesitate as they approached a home overflowing with people. Above the man's head, they quietly discussed what they ought to do as they drew closer to the door. Even from his vantage point he could see that there were so many people that the doorway was blocked. All he could detect were a variety of coloured robes as neighbours stood shoulder to shoulder, attempting to edge their way in closer. His friends tried to entreat people to make way for him, but their words didn't have much impact. No one was moving. Rather, they were shushed as the crowd strained forward, as though trying to hear a voice inside.

There was no way in. They were blocked from seeing this Jesus. The man gazed up at the sky, battling mixed emotions. Relief with dismay. Longing with fear and doubt. Although hope had crept in as they'd travelled here, he didn't believe he deserved this attention. Before long, the familiar, resigned dullness fell on him. It was time to go back. To return to the same hopeless, dark, and fearful situation.

He didn't notice at first, but he soon realized that his friends weren't giving up. They made their way around the house seeking another doorway or entrance. He sensed their urgency and their dogged determination as they inquired of one and then another about a way in. All the while they held his bed firmly in their strong hands—fishermen and carpenter hands. How bold and faithful they were.

Then the first man gave a triumphant cry. "The roof!" Another of his friends laughed in agreement. Before he could protest, the man found himself swaying on an angle as his friends resolutely carried him up the outer stairs of the home. The roof? Fear and shame rose in him. They were going to get to Jesus through the roof? With neighbours and Scribes watching? He studied the hands of these four friends. Maybe they still couldn't get him to Jesus. Given the determination on their faces, though, he knew they would. Hope mixed into the fear again.

And then the question slammed into him—what would he do when he met Jesus? How could it be that a mere human would receive this confidence and trust? Authority from God? Who was He, this man who healed all who came to Him? He hardly dared imagine being healed. He had imagined it, years ago, but had long given up. It wasn't possible. Or, was it? In spite of the disjointed thoughts whirling through his mind, his friends remained undaunted in their conviction and their mission. This man, Jesus, would heal him. They only had to get their friend to Him.

The group of friends reached the rooftop. They set the mat down flat on the plastered surface and began an animated discussion on their next step. The man lay there listening to their passion, and his heart was stirred. What would happen now? Was he ready? He peered helplessly through his eyelashes, witnessing the ferocious way these men tackled that roof, pulling at the mud plaster, throwing the debris behind them. To him, it felt as though they were gouging out the barrier to faith. They would not be stopped. With every moment that passed, every chunk of clay plaster that flew through the air to land with a thud, the man became more and more aware of his helplessness, his need, his fears, his darkness. They weighed on him, pressing him to that rooftop, insisting that nothing could be done.

Yet, below was Jesus.

The whispered conversation of his friends broke through some of the shadows.

"Pull a bit more on this side first…"

"Oh no! The Pharisees are right below. We're getting dust on them."

"Keep going."

"Jesus glanced up. Was that a smile on His face?"

"All right, I think the hole is big enough."

Before he was ready, the man's friends gathered around him, bending to reach the leather straps.

"Here we go, friend!"

Panic overtook him, and he protested in a harsh whisper, "No! I can't go down. Don't lower me in front of all those people. Maybe Jesus doesn't want to see me. No. *No.* Pull me back up!"

His companions ignored his fears. "You'll see," one of them replied calmly.

And with a lurch, he swung over the opening, staring at the sky, momentarily suspended. He shut his eyes tightly for a few seconds, trying to pray. Nothing. He opened his eyes and shifted his attention to the four faces. Confident faces, filled with care and mercy. One of his friends winked at him, and another nodded encouragement. His heart lifted with possibility, even as it battled the terror of the unknown. Then, as he was lowered slowly, rocking slightly, the sky disappeared. His friends peered past him, smiling at someone below.

Their muscles strained as, lying flat on the roof, they stretched out their arms, clay dust floating through the air in the beams of sunlight. Other faces came into view around him. Neighbours all standing, their faces filled with anticipation and wonder. Dark robed men, some with pinched looks, sat near Jesus. Dust had settled on them, undermining their dignified appearance.

Overwhelmed by the attention, the man turned his head. His gaze settled on and was immediately captured by eyes that carried so much love and compassion he could hardly breathe. This man, this Rabbi, knew what he had done. All of it.

It must be Jesus. A slight smile on his face, the Healer tipped His head back and nodded at the men peering down through the hole in the roof. Then He turned to the man, lying weakly on the floor of the home, and spoke a word filled with mercy and compassion. "Son."

As the man gazed into Jesus' eyes, filled with warmth, his longing for a Father's acceptance rose up. Tears filled his eyes.

"Your sins are forgiven." Authority pierced the silence.

The man exhaled. Forgiven? All he had done was released and gone? All the ways he felt as though he had missed the mark, no longer for him to carry? Forgotten? A deep relief settled in his heavy heart as the truth sank in. A sob rose in his throat as his eyes filled. Somehow those words of great mercy and grace penetrated into his dark heart and freed him from fear and shame. They offered greater freedom than he would have experienced if his legs suddenly worked. This freedom was enough to revel in. Joy bubbled up with the sob.

Jesus lifted His head to stare at the scholars. With piercing eyes and a clear voice, the Rabbi said to the dust-covered Pharisees, "Why do you debate these things in your hearts and minds and so create confusion?" His gaze flickered back to the man. "Which do you think is an easier thing, to say to the paralytic, 'Your every sin is taken care of' or to say, 'Rise up and walk'?"

The paralytic, taking in the words of Jesus, felt the full weight of the Healer's eyes, now filled with a fierce desire to heal. He heard Him declare, through the lightness of forgiven sins, "But that you may understand in your hearts that the Son of Man has this kind of power on earth to cover all sin, rise. Roll up that mat of yours and go home."

Heat and strength flowed through the man's limbs. Without letting a questioning thought enter his mind, he sprang to his feet in response to the words of power. No longer weak in frame and with a heart full of boldness before the crowd, he bent over and rolled his mat up for the first time, gathering up the stray straps under his restored arms. With growing confidence and strength, he paused in wonder before weaving his way through the crowd on legs still filled with heated power. Before the startled Pharisees, the astonished faces of his neighbours, and the murmurings of awe and shock and reverent worship to God, he absorbed the wonder of a completely healed body.

The man pushed through the door frame that had previously been a barrier. His four exultant friends rushed around the corner of the house. They grabbed him in bear hugs he could now feel, slapping him on the back while calling out praise to the God who forgives and heals.

When they could finally bring themselves to let him go, they returned to his home with joy.

FAITH NURTURED

For I, the Lord your God,
hold your right hand;
it is I who say to you, "Fear not,
I am the one who helps you.

—Isaiah 41:13

"Come quickly, dear friend. The Rabbi is approaching Bethsaida." The urgent voices of the man's neighbours and friends grew closer until he sensed them rushing into his small home.

Strong, cool hands grasped both of his, pulling him to his feet from the place he'd been reclining near the wall. The Rabbi? Nearby? He could not have anticipated that would happen this day.

"Let's go. We will ask Him to touch your eyes and you will see. It is what He does."

The dull pain behind his eyes increased. The shadows in his sight shifted from dark to a murky light as, familiar with his home, he ducked his head beneath the doorframe and entered the daylight. He knew of this Healer and bread-multiplier. They called Him Jesus. People had streamed by the blind man's home, whispering in awed voices about the abundance of bread and fish the Rabbi had provided the thousands of people who were following Him. Perhaps they could have found food on their own, but He gave it out of His own hands. This wondrous sign had happened so close, but the man hadn't been there that day as it was nearly impossible to navigate crowds without help.

Two of his friends tugged on his arms, drawing his attention back to their urgency as they expertly navigated the roadway with him. They discussed the best route to take and whether they would be on time, but the man's mind again wandered to this Jesus who taught with conviction and healed with ease. So many stories had filtered his way about this Teacher and Healer, as his friends shared every snippet they heard. They even told him a rumour of a man born blind being healed at His touch. Born blind and now seeing. The wonder!

Could he also see again? Did he believe this man could touch him and heal him? He hadn't witnessed a single miracle, although the stories did inspire hope. But did he deserve this? He wasn't a good man. Wasn't even always law-abiding, as it was nearly impossible to meet all the requirements of the law. As he contemplated that and what the leaders would say about him, hope died. Yet, his friends' chatter was filled with the confidence that he would receive his sight. Oh, to see again! How long had it been? And to be free from pain. Dare he hope?

The terrain changed under his feet, and his friends became more urgent. They were close to the village of Bethsaida. The air carried the moist salty air of the sea and the smell of fish. When was the last time he'd ventured this far?

Why was he doing so now, simply to meet this Rabbi? What if nothing happened? Would it be his fault?

Sounds and nudges increased around him, suggesting that the crowd was growing thicker as they approached the village. His friends pushed and manoeuvred him through the people competing for space, somehow managing to protect him as they did. They were good friends. Accepting of him. Their desire for his healing brought a secret longing to the surface. Oh, to see again!

The sounds and smells of the marketplace grew more evident as the threesome hurried along. They paused every so often to inquire about where the Rabbi Jesus might be. Word had spread about Him, and a number of people seemed knowledgeable about where He was. Still, the blind man sensed something missing. Maybe it was the caution in the merchants' voices as they talked of this Rabbi.

Soon the crowds seemed to be thinning. One of the man's friends exclaimed, "I see Him. There He is!" More confidence in their steps now, his companions grasped the man's arms and wove around a few more bodies before stopping.

"Please, Rabbi. Please, Jesus. Please touch our friend. He is blind." The man could hear the passion and confidence in his dear friends' voices. They sounded as though they knew Jesus could heal him. No, *would* heal him. Could he share that confidence? Desire and hope welled up in his heart.

A touch interrupted this introspection as a calloused hand took hold of his. A tingle spread through his fingers and up his arm. This must be Jesus! Rather than touching his eyes, as the man expected, the Rabbi gently tugged on his hand, encouraging him to follow. The man hesitated briefly then followed.

Questions rose, swirling in the air around him, echoing his. As the calloused hand guided his steps, dark thoughts chased him. Fearful and insistent. After some time the noise and chatter grew quieter. The blind man sensed that they were heading outside the village. Was no one following them? When it was quiet, they stopped. The air filled with expectancy, as though something new was about to happen. Dare he trust this man? He had to admit that there was something compelling about Him.

Now alone with Jesus, the man waited, head bowed.

A quiet sound broke the silence. Was that spitting? Something wet dripped over his eyes. He flinched. The Rabbi had spit on him! He battled shock. Warm hands pressed against his eyes. Again, the tingle, but greater than before and filling his eyes, moving through his body. Jesus removed His hands and gently asked, "How is your heart? Are you persuaded yet? What do you see?"

The blind man raised his head, his heart beating rapidly. Glancing around, he sensed his sight recovering and blinked. "I see people, but they look like trees, walking around." Hope and wonder rose inside him, competing with the questions.

Jesus put his hands on the man's eyes again, and he was overwhelmed by an infusing of power and love. His thoughts cleared. The questions vanished. With confidence in Jesus, he opened his eyes and stared intently, knowing the outcome. He saw people walking by clearly now. He saw the clear blue sea on a glorious day. Such blue!

Awe and gratefulness filled him. His gaze locked on Jesus' eyes, filled with a gentle love that washed over him. This man was more than a man, more than a rabbi and a healer. No mere man had such power and grace to gently lead him to his sight. No mere man had the mercy to not leave him in his questions but to bring him to this place of faith. And how astounding that Jesus desired to be alone with him so that His healing power could restore his sight.

His future now stretched out in a completely different direction than it had this morning when his friends dragged him out of his home. Different questions rose in his mind. Before he could even ask, Jesus answered them.

"Go home now. Avoid Bethsaida and go straight home."

The man, his vision and his heart both changed, was able to see everything in a whole new way. He was being sent out by the Son. Not back to his friends to tell them the good news but to his home to let all that he had seen and heard settle in his heart. They would hear soon enough.

Loosed

He sent out his word and healed them,
and delivered them from their destruction.

—Psalm 107:20

The woman was faithful. Every Sabbath she made her laborious way to the synagogue. She knew her path well, which helped, but the people around her were unpredictable. Each of her steps was carefully placed to avoid every stone and dip in the path. She braced herself along the wall, measuring her progress by the changing texture. People brushed by, often bumping into her as she was easily overlooked until it was too late. When they jostled her, the woman's back would ache even more, and it was hard to hold back the tears.

The synagogue was close now—she could feel the incline in the ache in her legs. And the feet within her view all travelled in the same direction. Finally, the smooth stone ahead indicated that she should abandon the bracing wall and venture across the open space to the synagogue's doorway. The sun fell warm on her back as she took her measured steps, craning her head sideways to spot her final destination. As she drew closer, a kind hand on her back guided her along the final steps to the entrance of the synagogue and the women's section.

When she reached the designated area, she found her corner and leaned against the wall to catch her breath, staring at the stone floor and listening to the hushed murmurings around her.

The woman was content to listen and rest. Others often felt uncomfortable speaking to her when it required crouching to meet her eyes. Most wouldn't remember her when she'd been able to stand tall with shoulders back. Somewhere along the way life began filling with disappointments and loss and the weight slowly bent her over. Now she had no idea how to get out from under it.

Voices quieted at the familiar rustle of the synagogue ruler's robes as he moved to his position. No doubt all eyes except for hers were on him. The sound of scrolls being unrolled and sacred words being read washed over her, a comfort in her pain and weariness. Then a new voice began reading the Torah. A visiting Rabbi? Whoever He was, He spoke with great authority. The words filled the room with excitement as He ended the reading and began to teach. Was this the man she'd been hearing about? The one who gave bold messages and healed the sick and lame? If only she could see Him. Ah, but it hurt too much to even straighten up enough to see those in front of her.

A long pause followed the teaching. In the silence the woman could imagine the Rabbi looking around the room wanting the people to understand. Her heart beat faster and stronger with the life and hope this man's words carried. They were different, somehow, than any she had heard before.

Suddenly, the Rabbi raised His voice and spoke with assurance. "Woman! You are loosed from your infirmity."

Though she was hidden in the far corner, seeking to be inconspicuous, she *knew* He spoke to her. Robes rustled again and bodies shifted as footsteps approached. The woman's body tensed. She sensed a battle inside, or was it outside of her? A malevolent force being exposed. One that had pressed her spine down and doubled her over for so long. The pressure increased as the man approached, until she nearly cried out. And then… His hands touched her back. A gentle pressure and immediately an electrical energy sent life flowing through her spine. The dark presence left. The woman felt weightless and immediately straightened without effort. Light and free. Loosed. No longer bound tight with pain and memories.

Joy burst out of her. Joy and freedom and… something else. What was it? Love. Such love that washed everything away. She couldn't contain her joy and praise. Glory to God poured out of her mouth as she lifted her hands and looked up to heaven. For the first time in eighteen years she could stand tall before her Maker and show Him her face. She turned to this Man as awed whispers filled the air around her, voices whispering His name. Jesus. She took in His countenance, one of peace and authority. She knew that authority now. She'd felt it in His touch. She'd heard it in His command.

Then, cutting through her joy and praise and ease of standing, burst a strident voice. The ruler of the synagogue indignantly spoke to the crowd, including the woman in his glance. "There are six days for working. Come on those days to be healed. Don't come on the Sabbath!"

Always faithful to obey the law as well as she could, the woman's face flushed at the suggestion that she was breaking the Sabbath law. Had she, unintentionally, broken the Sabbath? But, as condemnation threatened her, she looked at this Rabbi who had touched her. His face bore the look of flint as He glared at the ruler.

"Hypocrites! You say one thing and do another. Don't you, on the Sabbath, set free your animals from the manger and lead them to water so they can drink? This woman is a daughter of Abraham and has been tied up by Satan for eighteen long years. Shouldn't she be loosed from this bond of affliction on the Sabbath and receive what she needs?"

As the words echoed in the synagogue the final fears and aches vanished from her heart, like wisps of smoke blown away by the wind. All condemnation fled. The ruler and those around him dropped their gazes. They gathered their robes and swept out of the synagogue while the crowd around her murmured with excitement and joy at this man's message.

The woman gazed upon her Healer and saw love and acceptance in His eyes, before He, too, turned and left. This Rabbi had been able to cut through all that held her in bondage, command Satan, and set her free. Joy again bubbled from her lips, and she joined the rejoicing crowd as they welcomed her eagerly.

The Cleansing

For I will restore health to you,
and your wounds I will heal,
declares the Lord,
because they have called you an outcast:
'It is Zion, for whom no one cares!'

—Jeremiah 30:17

The man wrapped his cloak around himself tighter, adjusting the special headpiece over his face as he tucked himself closer to the tree. Those on the road from the hillside beyond to the nearby town all seemed to walk with purpose. Some laughed and others were silent in their travels. Many smiled and a good number frowned. None of them were the one he was looking for, though.

The man adjusted his position, hoping he hadn't been noticed. He was a long way from home, but he'd heard of the man who healed. He had tried once before to approach the Rabbi after he observed others going to Him, being touched, and leaving rejoicing. Even from a distance he could see that this Healer was unusual. Although the man wanted what the Rabbi had, he wasn't sure he was ready to brave the crowds and their aversion to him. Besides that, he had to announce his coming for all to hear, which took a lot out of him. The law required it, but still, it cost him a great deal to bare his shame before all.

The burden of his sin and disease was eating at him even inside his heart. He missed his family, though they'd had no choice but to reject him. The Law called for it. Something fierce rose inside him, something that told him this man was hope. But would He really want to heal someone like him? The man who must have committed some grave sins to have contracted this terrible disease? The sores eating at his flesh were proof of his unrighteousness. He wasn't worthy of a touch. He wasn't fit to belong.

Yet, here he was, hiding and waiting. The disease had advanced and desperation grew inside him. Reports of the Healer had continued to drift even to those hidden from society. Reports of a Rabbi—he recalled that His name was Jesus—who restored and healed with only a touch or a word. He was tired of hiding. In his desperation he had crept out last night to make his way to where the latest rumours hinted at the Rabbi's location.

The man scanned the sloping road winding around the hills in the distance. A crowd came toward him following a man. Could it be? He'd heard crowds were growing as the Rabbi travelled from town to town. A crowd. He shrank behind a tree. That meant too many people for one who must separate himself. But he couldn't bring himself to leave. Instead, he fixed his eyes on the progress of the man leading the crowd.

Slowly the throngs made their way down the hillside, dust floating in the air around them as they drifted closer to his hiding spot. He tugged his cloak down over his disfigured face and slid his hands into the folds of the cloth, trying to hide his stumps of fingers. His heart pumped furiously and his face flushed with longing as he battled the fear of rejection.

As this Healer came nearer the man began hearing whispers of the name, "Jesus". *It is him*. Would the Rabbi heal a man like him? Somehow the man knew He could. But would He? He'd heard too many stories of what He was able to do for the broken and diseased to doubt his power. Still, the man was unclean. And this Rabbi seemed pure and good.

As the Rabbi drew closer, the man studied his face through the branches. Kindness and goodness appeared to surround him like the cloak surrounded the diseased man. He seemed safe. When the man sensed the timing was right, he rushed out of his hiding place and made his way to the edge of the road. He fixed his eyes on Jesus as He walked the few steps toward him. His heart continued to pound as if it would come out of his chest. Belief and shame. Fear and faith. He was so nervous he forgot to cry out his presence. Could he have gotten out the cry of "Unclean! Unclean!" if he had remembered?

Before he could desperately fall to his knees at Jesus' feet, a suppressed cry came out of him. Head bowed and frozen in place, not daring to look at this Healer's goodness, the words tore out of the man, "If you will, You can make me clean."

A hand rested on his shoulder. The man gasped. *A touch?* The weight of compassion and love like he'd not felt in years settled over him. His heart lifted in expectation.

A voice strong with confidence and authority rang out. "It is my desire to heal you. Be clean."

Clean! The touch and the words washed over him. Energy and heat and love and power swept over his body—over his nose, his fingers, his toes. So many sensations came to life in his flesh that he was almost overwhelmed. He could almost feel the empty, dark shame of the disease leaving his body. The warmth filled his heart, driving away every cut and wound of rejection and every announcement of his shame over the years.

The man eagerly pulled back his sleeves to examine hands he hadn't seen in years. Complete fingers. Smooth skin. He yanked the cloak from his face so he could feel it with those fingers. Whole. Slowly he lowered his arms and, his face uncovered, turned to look at his Healer. Eyes filled with acceptance and sparkling with joy greeted him. Jesus threw back his head and laughed, obviously delighted at the healing.

As if from a distance, wonder still swirling around him, the man heard Jesus speak the words every leper longed to hear, "Go show yourself to the priest and offer what Moses commanded for your cleansing as proof to them." Cleansing and acceptance were now his. He could go home. Home! The thought of holding his wife and children again nearly overwhelmed him.

Joy filled the man's heart until he couldn't contain it. No longer hunched under his cloak he stood tall and, like Jesus, threw back his head with laughter before crying out, "I am clean. Jesus has made me clean!"

Restored

Behold, I am doing a new thing;
now it springs forth, do you not perceive it?
I will make a way in the wilderness
and rivers in the desert.

—Isaiah 43:19

The man sat on the cool flagstone of the synagogue, settling into his usual spot. The stone chilled the man now,
but he knew that, as the room filled with people and the heat
from the sun drifted in, he would be thankful for the refreshing
temperature through his robe. He tried to get comfortable as
he waited for various neighbours and familiar faces to find their
places on this sacred day. His mind flitted to fearful thoughts
as a twinge shot through his hand. He rubbed it, cradling it on
his lap as he fiercely directed his attention to the decorated box
that held the Torah. What would Yahweh say about his situation—the one that continually plagued his mind?

A pillar shielded him from the few empty chairs that
sat in the front of the synagogue next to the sacred Torah.
Those seats waited for important people with drapery-like
robes. They'd sweep into the synagogue shortly, he was sure.
Somehow one of those important faces would find him with

an intent look, even with the pillar between them. He dreaded the censure. It stirred up what was in his heart.

More people entered the synagogue and found places either on the benches or the mats on the floor. Several glanced his way before quickly averting their eyes. Were they avoiding sitting near him? What were they more afraid of catching— what he had or the attention of the Pharisees? Clearly they were all very aware of him sitting there. Their furtive glances never failed to heap shame and questions on his heart.

His focus shifted to his right hand lying limply in his lap, hidden under his outer cloak. Slowly, over the years, it had changed, weakening and becoming harder to use until he was unable to do his work. He began dropping threads and employment became impossible. Who wanted to hire someone with one hand? His skill as a weaver had been lost. Pride in a job well done? Gone. The ability to provide for his family, to do what his father had done and his father before that dried up. It was hard to meet the eyes of those he had let down. And there was no hope. The man rubbed his hand as another fearful twinge gripped it. He hid it because it looked different, withered. Though all in the village knew of it, he tried to make sure they didn't see it.

His hand was a symbol of loss and hopelessness. Of unanswered prayers. It represented all the doctors, medicine, massages, and oils that had given nothing in return for payment. Many openly offered advice of what to do about his ailment, but he also caught quietly spoken rumours that the leaders of the synagogue believed the deformity was the result of a hidden sin. Behind closed doors people murmured that it was his fault. Their judgment weighed on him. His heart felt dry and dark. Regrets he had long forgotten now shot their darts at him throughout each day. How could he fight his sin and his past mistakes?

Did he want to be here, surrounded by eyes that held judgment? No. But he was still a man, and maybe one day a Torah reading would shed a little light on what was happening. Surely there were answers? A sliver of comfort, even from a silent God?

The room filled up as the faithful trickled in and found seats on the flagstone and the surrounding benches. The distinct rustle of rich robes quieted the whispered conversation in the room. Everyone watched the dignified leaders find their spots. One rose and the service began as he closed his eyes and recited the Shema.

As the final words faded in the synagogue a shift happened in the air. Pulled from his thoughts, the man opened his eyes and glanced around the room. Others did the same. His gaze stopped on a group of men who had entered in coarse robes and with soft, sandaled steps. Murmurs and a strange hum of excitement grew in the room as everyone straightened. The men paused in the aisle. The man with the withered hand leaned forward to get a clearer look as whispers of "Jesus" and "the Rabbi" filled the air. This Jesus looked around the room until His gaze landed directly on him. His eyes were kind and full of compassion and they shimmered with anticipation.

The man shrank back on his mat. A stranger with gentle eyes that changed the atmosphere and elicited a flurry of hushed comments had spotted him. Did everyone, even this Jesus, know of his shame? He sat a bit straighter as the Rabbi walked calmly to the front of the synagogue. He wasn't impressive in stature, but He walked with authority and confidence. The man, even from his vantage point, had caught the spark of purpose in Jesus' eyes before He turned to face the heavily robed leaders. The leaders watched Him very closely, as if waiting to see what He would do. Obviously they knew this man and they were challenged by Him. That the haughty leaders could be wary of anyone was almost more than the man could comprehend.

Jesus shifted his attention to the congregation of villagers. A few of the leaders shifted in their chairs, their frowns deepening. The Rabbi's gaze fell again on the man, partially hidden in his spot at the back of the synagogue. His heart pounded at the attention and at the awareness of the fury growing on the leaders' faces. Then Jesus spoke to him, the soft words reaching the man as from a distance.

"Come and stand here." The command, spoken with a compelling gentleness, was for him. He searched the Rabbi's face and found no judgment, only that unpitying compassion. The man stood as whispers rose and bodies shifted to make room. He kept his eyes on the Rabbi as he made his way to Him, carefully keeping his withered hand hidden in his robes. Questions swirled in his mind, mingling with the ever present shame and fear. What would happen now?

This man saw him. Not his hand but him. No censure, but still a knowing. Jesus perceived what had brought him to this point in his life. And as the man stopped in front of Jesus and their eyes met he saw… love? Yes. Love and determination and purpose. For him. And the man stood a bit straighter, as if a little of the shame was falling off his shoulders.

Then Jesus, with a hand on the man's shoulder, turned to those at the front and said, "I ask you, is it permitted to do that which is good or evil, is it permitted to save life or destroy it?" His gaze swept across the people congregated there. Many who had been staring at the man with the deformity lowered their eyes.

Jesus' gaze found the man's again. When he spoke, authority and life were woven through his voice. "Stretch out your hand."

His right hand. The one hidden. The one hugged to his body in fear. His symbol of shame and helplessness. Stretch it out, in front of his neighbours? In front of all those who shunned and barely tolerated him? Bring it out before the leaders, whose fury was growing on their faces?

Suddenly, he didn't care about any of that. He was standing with a man who possessed a love and life and power that infused hope and faith. He knew this Man could be trusted like no other rabbi. With eyes fixed on Jesus he pulled his hand from its hiding place, exposing it to all eyes in the room. When he heard the gasps he looked down to find his hand fully restored, looking like it had years ago when he could still weave! In wonder he attempted to move it and, now strong and healthy, it obeyed his commands. What had been destroying his hand was now itself destroyed! His shame evaporating, the man looked around the room.

Filled with wonder and delight, he turned back to Jesus. The Healer's eyes were alight with mirroring delight. The gaze that met his was filled with such a love that it washed over the man and removed the last remnants of guilt and regret. His past was gone. His present challenges had been overcome, all taken care of by one Rabbi.

Released from Silence

The voice of the Lord is powerful;
the voice of the Lord is full of majesty.
The voice of the Lord breaks the cedars;

—Psalm 29:4,5a

He wandered the lower hills overlooking the Sea of Galilee. The waving grass was lush and dotted with pink flowers. Here the silence didn't matter as much. The morning breezes tantalized his face, and the colours filled his eyes. Here he was alone, and conversation didn't matter except for the thoughts in his heart as he enjoyed what Yahweh had created. At times he was sure he could hear Yahweh's voice whispering in his heart's ear. But who knew?

He mentally shrugged as he continued on the path toward his small town near the shores of the sea. In the distance fishing boats were scattered along the coast. The day was beautiful with a clear sky and the early morning sun sparkling like diamonds on the water's deep blue waves. Perfect for collecting a good night's haul. Though he couldn't hear them, the waving arms and eager movements of the fishermen in their boats indicated a good catch of fish. Pulling of nets began. Fish would be cleaned and sorted. A successful day for them.

He could spend all day here in his solitude, but it was time to go home, to tend to his day's tasks. As the man reluctantly and nimbly navigated the winding, rocky path, grasses, still slightly damp with dew, brushed his robe. He crested the rise and began the final downward slope to his home. A crowd had gathered outside the gates of his village. Though they were still off in the distance, his eyes were keen and he hesitated. A crowd was confusing and disorienting, and he wasn't ready for that. His heart started to pound with hints of dread, and the peace that had settled in his soul up in the hills seemed to wisp away on the same breezes that had comforted him. Peace was a fleeting thing.

The man paused on the narrow pathway. What should he do? Possibly the crowd would disperse shortly. He lived in the Decapolis, a region of 10 cities. Negotiating had to be done at the gates, so perhaps that was the excitement, and soon the different parties would go their separate ways. Maybe if he waited…

His mind was made up when he saw a man and a woman farther down the path waving at him as if they had sought him out. Their robes fluttered in the breeze and the woman's garment caught on a nearby bush. That they knew how to find him on this, one of many hillside paths, showed that they were familiar with his solitary morning habits. Why were they looking for him? The man slowly continued on the path, still reluctant but curious. He was willing to try to communicate with this couple to find out what they wanted and what was going on. Better here without the busy crowd.

The woman had freed herself, and as he drew closer he saw it was the couple that lived right beside him and kept a protective watch on him. They weren't intrusive but careful to help when they saw a need. Their kindness was evident in their patience, but at the moment they were clearly excited. The woman's eyes were alight with purpose and expectation, and the man could no longer wait for him to get near but jogged toward him, gripping his arm with the clear intent of pulling him quicker down the path. Facing him directly and using hand motions, they managed to explain that they wanted to take him to a man. That was all he could make out.

The silence screamed louder as he tried hard to pay attention to the hand motions and the lips and understand more of what they were saying. Finally, they started toward the city and he followed them, trusting their urgency but frustrated that he couldn't understand it—a familiar emotion.

As he was tugged down the familiar path toward his town, he battled frustration with his silent world. Mixed with that emotion was the weariness of pushing through the lack of hearing daily. His condition had begun as a child when, over time, his hearing diminished. More and more each year. Words became increasingly difficult to express, as he couldn't figure out how to form his tongue around new words. As he retreated further into silence out of fear, he lost what little he did know. It was as if a band was wrapped around his tongue, hindering it, paralyzing it. He longed to join in conversations, but it was too challenging and, given the difficulty with communicating, friendships became harder and harder to navigate. After a few years his silence was complete. Little could penetrate his solitary world except the rugged beauty of these hills and these kind neighbours. So, he followed them.

The man soon realized the crowd outside the town gates wasn't a delegation for civic negotiations. It was too informal and diverse. Robes and ages of all kinds. Though the town gates were to the east of his path, the crowd was facing towards the Sea to the west. With practiced eyes used to observing people in his silence, he scanned both familiar and strange faces. Many in the crowd wore expectation, like his neighbours who were insistently drawing him closer to their goal. Joy and tears could be seen on some faces, curiosity on others, and a hunger for more on the rest. Most were patiently listening, attention fixed on a man. But the deaf man could sense need and urgency in others, matching what he sensed in his neighbours. He glanced at them before spotting the young man, ordinary in appearance but evidently known to many in this crowd. His silent world had made him unaware of who this man was. Though that was more by choice. While frustrated with his lot in life, he had also grown strangely content with the rhythm of his days.

The couple gripped his arm as they wove through the press of people. It was clear their goal was this unusual man, and they were determined to not be stopped. They pushed through the crowd, ignoring any dark looks. What kind of man was this who not only commanded the attention of the people but also seemed to change them?

Before he could make up his mind about the man he was going to meet, he was standing in front of him, his arm still in the firm grip of his neighbour. The man who was looking at him, welcoming him, had the kindest eyes the deaf man had ever seen. Time slowed for a moment while those eyes searched his. Gradually he again became aware of the crowds of people around him, of his neighbours' mouths moving as they gestured animatedly to the man, of his town behind him and the Sea in front of him, of the distant hills and of his silence. His unceasing silence.

He jolted when the man, whom he now recognized as a rabbi, took his arm in a strong hand and strode away from the crowd. He sensed purpose in the grip, and a shiver of anticipation rippled through him. They walked along one of the many paths leading to the hills above the Sea. Though the silence in his head stifled him, their surroundings vibrated with life—waving grasses and flowers, birds floating in the sky, and the now calm Sea. When they were far from the crowd, both strangers and neighbours, they stopped. The deaf man stood alone, facing the mysterious Rabbi, yet he felt no fear, only growing anticipation.

What the Rabbi did next shocked him. He lifted both hands and gently inserted a finger in each of the man's ears for a moment. When he removed them, the Rabbi spit on His fingers, gently opened the man's mouth, and touched his tangled tongue. Puzzled but with the trickle of anticipation growing, the man watched as the Rabbi lifted His eyes to the blue sky of heaven. His chest lifted and He slowly heaved out a large sigh as if from great pressure. Confused, the deaf man focused on the Rabbi's lips. They moved to utter a single word that he interpreted as "Open!"

A surge of heat and an explosive tingling rushed into his ears. The man's eyes widened as the splashing of water, murmurs of distant voices, and notes of a bird song cascaded into his ears like waves crashing against the shore. Before he could revel in the joys of the sounds of the hills, that mysterious heat and tingling filled his mouth. His stiffened tongue loosened in a way he couldn't remember experiencing, moving in a way he knew instinctively formed words.

Joy overwhelmed him. The heat and tingling faded and he gazed in wonder at his Healer. The warm eyes that met his twinkled. For a moment, the man didn't move. Then voices filled the air behind him. He turned to his friends, calling out with joy and words that came out right.

Their faces lit up as they recognized that healing and restoration had happened. They ran toward him calling out, "Jesus, be praised! Glory to the Lord!"

Before they reached the two of them, the man turned back to the Rabbi, seeking out the kind eyes that appeared full of joy but tired, as though he had just exerted a great amount of energy.

"Jesus?" the man asked. "You are Jesus?"

A quiet nod from the Rabbi.

The man bowed his head before Him and, with tears gathering, spoke the words he longed to say, "Thank you."

An arm from behind him pulled him into a fierce hug. His neighbour peered over his shoulder to say to Jesus, with laughter in his voice, "You have done all things well, Jesus! You have made my deaf and mute friend hear and speak. You have released him from his silence. We will now find out what this quiet friend has been thinking all these years. Thank you!"

The twinkle in Jesus' eyes turned into quiet laughter that blended with the wind, waves, and birds behind him.

HONOUR SAVED

Before they call I will answer;
while they are yet speaking I will hear.

—Isaiah 65:24

The joy was thick and pulsing in the air. The wedding was rich with smells and sounds that reflected that joy. Hints of lamb and mint wafted in the air. A few short days ago the bride had been brought here amid a festive torchlight procession. So began the young couple's wedding week.

Short in stature, the young man strode across the stone floor, weaving through the well- dressed crowd to the back of the torch lit courtyard where another jar filled with wine was waiting to be exchanged with his empty one. His role was to serve wine to the numerous guests. The wedding had drawn family members and Cana's community alike, so his feet had flown as he'd made sure the wine was always there for parched throats and happy hearts alike. This bride and groom held a special place in the hearts of the villagers, and the gladness of the guests was genuine. There was nothing like wine to show that gladness and give honour to the union of the new couple. Love and warmth flowed through the celebrations making his demanding task a pleasure.

The food kept coming even on this third day of the week-long feasting, and the man paused to tap his feet to the music. Guests whirled over the floor, light shimmering on their faces. His feet itched to join out of love for the groom and his new bride, but it wasn't his place. He glanced at the master of the feast to see if he had observed his momentary lapse. He was known to be too much of a thinker for a servant, and it sometimes got him in trouble. Thankfully, he didn't see a frown on the feast master's face.

He caught the eye of his friend and fellow servant who had also been tasked with serving wine to the guests. His friend's brows were gathered in a frown. His stout friend was a more serious sort, so perhaps he wasn't enjoying the festivities as much as the young man was. He continued on his path to retrieve another jar but stopped short when he reached the courtyard. No wine jar waited for him. Scanning the area, he spotted his friend huddled with another servant and whispering with agitated gestures of his arm.

In concern, he moved closer to hear the animated conversation. Distress filled his friend's voice as he hissed, "What should we do? There's no more wine."

The man's eyes widened. No wine? That would bring shame on the family and disgrace on the bride and groom. One could not fully honour a wedding and a union without wine, and there was still half a week left to celebrate. What could have happened? His friend bore the same look of helplessness on his face that he was sure he did. The music grew painfully loud behind them.

Interrupting their thoughts, an elegant woman, simply dressed, approached with gentle concern on her face. Mary of Nazareth. She had moved to Cana recently and had quickly become friends with the family, even helping with some of the details of the wedding. The servants hid their panic quickly so as to not reveal the problem to one of the guests. But she was clearly not fooled. "I sense there is a problem," she said with a gentle smile.

The man's friend burst out, "There's no wine! The master of the feast isn't aware of it yet, but we are trying to figure out what to do."

A thoughtful look crossed Mary's face as she contemplated the festive crowd. The man clutched the empty wine jar under his arm and followed her gaze. Not far from where the servants stood, a young man milled about with several other men at one of the side entrances. Jesus. Mary's son. Stories had preceded him here of how He was gathering followers and they had now arrived at the wedding.

Mary approached her son, who was clearly enjoying the laughter and camaraderie between Himself and a few other guests. She laid a hand on His arm and leaned close to whisper something to Him. The man couldn't hear what she said, but Jesus nodded and He and His mother, along with a small group of men, approached the gathered servants.

Mary smiled again at the servants as the group approached them. Looking at her son, she simply stated, "They have no wine."

The young servant was somehow not surprised at her revealing this to her son, even though the honour of the family was at stake. He studied them both. How could she look at her son so calmly and with such an air of expectancy?

Jesus' reply, though respectful, was unexpected. "Dear woman, what does any of this have to do with me? My season hasn't started." The servant blinked. Wasn't this woman his mother?

The servant observed her slightly hurt reaction, eyes widening as she took in His reply. The disciples shifted a bit behind Him as they took in the exchange. Mary recovered her calm expression and, with a slight smile on her face, she turned to the servants. "Do whatever he tells you." Then she inclined her head gracefully and left to rejoin the festivities, soon engaging a guest in conversation.

The servant contemplated Jesus, pondering His response to His mother. Jesus' face reflected the concern of one who wanted to intervene and could but on His own timing. He could sense that this man wasn't being swayed by his mother's instructions to the servants as much as by the honour and need of the bridal couple, even if they weren't aware of that need yet. Tilting his head, he waited to see what Jesus would say.

"Fill the jars with water," was His quiet command as He indicated six jars standing neatly on a bench that lined the wall. The limestone jars were intended for purification of the guests, but they stood empty now, having been used when the festivities began. The servant shot a look at his friend who was frowning a bit more than normal. For some reason, he felt an inner compelling to obey.

Nudging another servant, he waved his hand to encourage him to follow, and the two made their way to the stone jars. His friend followed behind and the three of them carried the heavy containers to the well behind the courtyard. They'd done this many times before, and they fell into their routine. The young servant was filled with anticipation as he made sure the jar was filled to the brim. It didn't matter how heavy it would be, he knew he needed to put as much liquid in as he could. The water bubbled as they filled each jar, and he enjoyed its refreshing spray in the remaining heat of the evening. The full jars were carried over and placed on the bench next to the empty jars, and those were quickly taken to do the same. Soon six jars sat full of fresh water from the well, and the servants stood next to them waiting for the next command.

Jesus smiled as He left a quiet conversation with His companions and walked over to the servants. "Now pour a glass and serve it to the master of the feast."

Take water to the master? The servants exchanged a look, but Jesus' eyes twinkled, and He spoke with such uncommon authority that the young man again took the lead. He found a tray and a wine goblet and, grasping a ladle, walked over to the first stone jar of water. The liquid still shimmered but now with a strange hue. His friend took the ladle from him. After a surprised glance at the changed water, he dipped the ladle into the jar and poured the liquid into the goblet. The young man's mouth dropped open slightly. The water had turned auburn and a rich fragrance ascended from it, the heady aroma that indicated a superior wine. Excitement filled the young man's heart as he realized what this meant.

He took the tray and turned to look at Jesus. Eyes warm and brown and filled with compassion met his. Wonder filled the servant's heart. Wine from water. Honour from shame. What man was this that He could create something so extravagant from something so common?

Jesus nodded and the servant clutched the tray as he headed to the festivities to find the feast master. When he spotted him at his post chatting with a guest he picked up his pace a little, eager to serve the master the wine. The other servants hurried along behind him.

When the servant stopped in front of him and held out the tray with the single goblet, the master of the feast raised an eyebrow. The young servant bowed slightly. "For you to taste, Sir."

He watched the feast master's face intently as he reached for the goblet of water, now become wine. He swirled it before lifting it to his mouth to taste. His eyes widened slightly as he held the liquid in his mouth before swallowing. He took another sip before lowering the goblet back to the tray. His gaze searched the crowd. The servants waited until he found the one he was looking for.

Off to the side of the musicians stood the tall bridegroom. The master approached and called him over to the servants bearing the wine. The bridegroom bent and whispered in his bride's ear. She blushed slightly. Even from a distance, the servant could see the love between the two. What a beautiful couple—now blessed by God and His show of mercy.

The bridegroom wove his way through the crowd of dancers and stopped before the master, a question in his eyes as he glanced at the tray. The master leaned in close to him. "This wine is outstanding! It is the best I've ever tasted." He waved a hand at the goblet. "Everyone shares their best wine at the beginning of the feast until everyone has drunk freely, but you have saved this most excellent wine until now."

After observing the surprise on the bridegroom's face, the servant nodded his respect to Jesus. Mary's son knew how to turn water into wine and how to magnify one's honour. What else did the young Rabbi have the power and compassion to do, and how many lives would he touch as a result?

The Story Behind the Stories

Dear Reader,

Digging into God's Word has been a passion of mine since a girl. Whether reading a devotional book, learning how the Bible is woven together, chasing down cross references, or discovering a Hebrew word in Scripture, I have earnestly sought the Lord in His Word through a variety of seasons of my life. He has used these means and more to reveal Himself to me. The need for His Word has been especially potent in times of crisis, in those times of desperate asking, seeking, and knocking. Those have been the seasons that have produced fruit.

During one of those times of need, a friend referred a particular pastor to me. His passion was teaching New Testament Scripture by exposing the Greek. I would often seek out the teaching from his website and podcasts. I would drink in these scholarly revelations of God's Word, amazed at what was hidden beneath my English version of the Scriptures. Then one day this pastor encouraged his listeners to look up the Greek in a lexicon ourselves. I started doing exactly that. I'd read a verse and explore the Greek gingerly, verb by verb and noun by noun. Often I would be in awe of what the Lord revealed in His words. This curiosity began to spill over to the Old Testament and the Hebrew. It was a journey that often provided surprises or confirmed something I sensed the Lord was showing me.

In this same, long season the desire to learn what the Bible said about physical healing grew. What was truly taught in the Bible on this topic? My search led me to dig into the Gospels for myself and to study the healings that Jesus performed. I started by studying Jesus' specific healings of the blind, applying what I had learned about the Greek. I printed out a copy of each gospel story in large font, including spaces between phrases for notes. Then, with a pencil and my mobile Greek Lexicon (found on an exhaustive app called *Bible Hub*), I'd highlight repeated phrases within each story and ferret out the meaning of the Greek. This treasure hunt yielded true treasure—but I had to hunt.

One winter day I was hiking in our woods, reflecting on what I was discovering and I sensed the Lord directing me to write the story of Blind Bartimaeus using what I had unearthed. That one story led me to dig for the treasure in another story and write that one. Over many months those stories grew into ten encounters with the young Rabbi, Jesus. This is what you hold in your hands right now.

May these stories be a touch from Jesus. A touch that changes you.

Annetta

Acknowledgements

My Father in Heaven whispered, beckoning me to write. Sometimes it took several tries to start, and other times the words poured out. He gave me the story "Bread Crumbs" in three hours. It's with heart overflowing that I acknowledge Him. These stories are for Him and I pray they reflect His love.

His Word is rich beyond measure. The simple tools and strategies I used revealed such treasure. I am grateful for His Book, and that I can live in it and feed on it whenever I desire to.

Thank you Paul, my husband and best friend. You are my greatest fan and cheerleader. You have celebrated this work of writing and have been faithful in battling in prayer for me. Thank you for listening well and urging me on.

Thank you Jadon, my delightful son. You love story. Your eager listening and insightful feedback have made my writing better.

And friends. What would raw writing be like if we couldn't share it with friends? Thank you Sarah for cheering me on from the beginning of this journey, and for encouraging my trust in His leading. And my friend, Sara, who read my stories in one sitting. You've known me for years and have no idea how valuable your faithful feedback is.

Rick Renner inspired my study of the Greek behind the Scriptural accounts of these ten stories and so gave depth to my imagination. I am grateful for his teaching about Jesus.

Roger Sapp's book added important layers to the writing of many of my stories. I am thankful for his work: *Performing Miracles and Healing – A Biblical Guide to Developing a Christ-Like Supernatural Ministry.*

Finally, my parents, who faithfully serve Jesus. Any endeavour or adventure of faith that Jesus has called me to, whether boldly or quietly, far or near, you have blessed with your support and prayers.